GASTON LEROUX

The Phantom of the Opera

Translated from the French
and retold by Stephen Colbourn

 MACMILLAN

Founding Editor: John Milne

The Macmillan Readers provide a choice of enjoyable reading materials for learners of English. The series is published at six levels – Starter, Beginner, Elementary, Pre-intermediate, Intermediate and Upper.

Level control
Information, structure and vocabulary are controlled to suit the students' ability at each level.

The number of words at each level:

Starter	about 300 basic words
Beginner	about 600 basic words
Elementary	about 1100 basic words
Pre-intermediate	about 1400 basic words
Intermediate	about 1600 basic words
Upper	about 2200 basic words

Vocabulary
Some difficult words and phrases in this book are important for understanding the story. Some of these words are explained in the story and some are shown in the pictures. From Pre-intermediate level upwards, words are marked with a number like this: ...³. These words are explained in the Glossary at the end of the book.

Contents

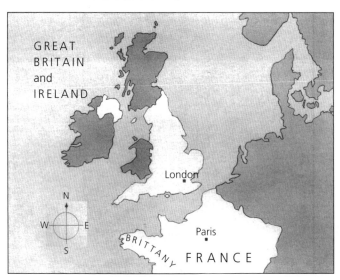

A Note About the Author

Gaston Leroux was French. He was born in Paris on 6th May 1868. His mother and father owned a clothes shop in Paris. Leroux was a lively boy. He liked literature and the theatre. Sometimes, he was in trouble with his parents and with the city officials.

Leroux studied to be a lawyer but he did not enjoy this work. Then his father died and Leroux got one million francs. The young man spent all the money in six months!

In 1890, Leroux became a reporter. He worked for the newspaper, *L'Echo de Paris*. He wrote about trials and criminals. He also wrote reports about plays in the theatres. His reports were clear and exciting. He became successful. Later, he was a journalist for the Paris newspaper, *Le Matin*.

Leroux was a big, heavy man. He had a large black beard. He liked fine clothes and good food and drink.

From 1894 to 1906, Gaston Leroux travelled to many countries. He wrote about wars and revolutions. He visited dangerous places. Many times, he had to put on unusual clothes and change his hair. Then he left these countries safely.

Leroux started to write stories and plays in the

1900s. In 1907, he stopped travelling. He did not work as a journalist. He did not write for newspapers. He wrote plays, poems and stories. He wrote adventure stories, romances, detective stories and horror stories. Some of his stories are: *The Mystery of the Yellow Room* (1907), *The Perfume of the Lady in Black* (1911), *The Man Who Came Back From the Dead* (1916), *The Secret of the Night* (1914) and *The Bride of the Sun* (1915). Leroux's most famous story, *The Phantom of the Opera*, was published in 1911.

Leroux died in Nice, France on 16th April 1927. He was 59 years old.

A Note About This Story

Time: 1880 to 1890.

Places: Brittany, and the Paris Opera House, France.

The Phantom of the Opera is a horror story.

Gaston Leroux visited the Paris Opera House many times. He liked the huge, beautiful building. He watched ballets. He listened to music and operas. Operas are musical plays. In an opera, the people on the stage do not speak – they sing.

The Opera House was built between 1861 and 1875. It is 167 m long, 122 m wide and 81 m high. It has 17 floors and a tall roof. There are 80 dressing-rooms for the actors, dancers and musicians. There are very many stairs, corridors and storerooms. In the

1900s, 1500 people worked in the building. Under the Opera House there were stables for horses. And there was a lake!

In 1910, Leroux heard some strange stories about the Opera House. The people of the Opera House talked about a ghost. The ghost lived in the building. Accidents had happened in the building too. Once, a huge glass chandelier fell from the ceiling. One woman died. Leroux thought about these things and he wrote his book.

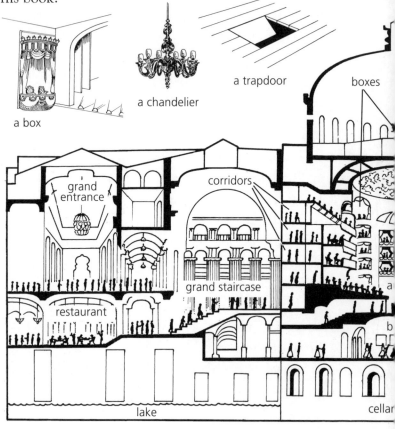

a box

a chandelier

a trapdoor

boxes

grand entrance

corridors

grand staircase

restaurant

a

b

lake

cellar

Many films and plays have been made of the story, *The Phantom of the Opera*. In 1925, there was an American film of the story. An actor called Lon Chaney was the Phantom. The film was very popular. In 1986, Andrew Lloyd-Webber wrote a musical play about the Phantom. Many thousands of people in London and New York have seen this musical.

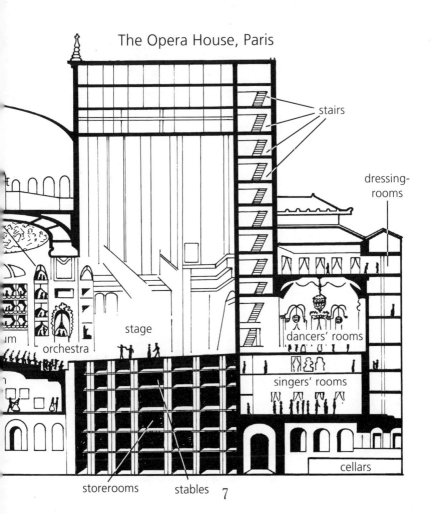

The Opera House, Paris

stairs

dressing-rooms

stage

orchestra

dancers' rooms

singers' rooms

cellars

storerooms   stables   7

The People in This Story

Philippe
fiːˈliːp

Raoul
raʊl

Christine
krɪsˈtiːn

Christine's father

The Persian

Erik
ˈɪrɪk

The Manager of the Opera House

Carlotta
kɑːrˈlɒta

Madame Richard
mædæm riːˈʃɑːr

1

The Angel of Music

The place was the coast of Brittany, in northern France. The time was a summer evening in 1880. Two people were sitting by the sea. They were sitting on a sandy beach, near an old church. They were a young girl and an old man. The girl was singing and the old man was playing a violin.

The young girl's name was Christine. The old man was her father. Christine and her father were travelling musicians. They travelled through all the countries of Europe. Sometimes, they performed music in hotels. Sometimes, they performed in the streets. Christine had a beautiful voice. In every country, people loved Christine's voice.

On that evening in 1880, Christine was looking at the sea. She was singing a sad song. It was a song about the sea, and about love. A man and a young boy were walking on the beach. They stopped near Christine and her father. They listened to the music.

The boy's name was Raoul. He was eleven years old. The man was Raoul's brother, Philippe. Philippe was much older than Raoul. He was thirty-one.

The two brothers stood near Christine and her father. Christine sang and her father played his violin. Raoul and Philippe listened to the music.

Christine was wearing a long blue scarf. Suddenly,

the wind blew the scarf from Christine's neck. The wind blew the scarf into the sea.

'I'll get your scarf,' said the young boy. 'Stay there. I'll bring it to you.'

'No, Raoul, No!' said Philippe. 'Don't go into the sea.'

But Raoul did not listen to his brother. He ran into the sea. He took the blue scarf from the water. He ran back to the beach and he gave the scarf to the young girl.

'Thank you,' said Christine. 'Thank you. I will always remember you.'

Raoul's clothes were wet. And Raoul's brother was angry.

'We must go home immediately,' Philippe said. 'You must put on some dry clothes.'

But Raoul did not want to go home. He wanted to
talk to the young girl.

'Will you sing a song for me?' Raoul asked Christine.

'Yes,' said Christine. 'Yes, I will sing for you.'

Again, the old man played the violin and Christine
sang. She sang a sad and beautiful song. It was a song
about love and about the stars.

'You have a beautiful voice,' said Raoul. 'You sing
very well.'

'My father teaches me very well,' said Christine.

'No, Christine,' said the old man. 'I am not a good teacher. You will have a better teacher soon.'

'Don't say that, father,' said Christine. 'You are a wonderful teacher.'

The old man spoke to Philippe and Raoul.

'Christine will have a better teacher,' he said. 'I will die soon. Then I will send a wonderful teacher to my daughter. I will send the Angel of Music to her.'

'Don't say that, please, father,' Christine said again.

But the old man said, 'Yes, Christine, I will die soon. I will send the Angel of Music to you.'

Suddenly, everybody heard a very beautiful sound. It was the sound of another violin. The sound came from the old church, near the beach.

Christine turned her head. Her eyes were shining. There were tears in her eyes.

'Oh,' she said. 'That is beautiful! Is that the Angel of Music?'

2

A Party at the Opera House

The Opera House in Paris is a huge building. There are hundreds of rooms. There are many corridors. And there are many cellars, deep under the stage.

One evening in 1890, the manager of the Opera House had a party. The party was in a very large room behind the stage of the Opera House.

Hundreds of people worked at the Opera House. Some people were singers and some people were dancers. Some people played musical instruments in the orchestra. Some people took care of the costumes. Some people took care of the lights. Some people moved the scenery on the stage. And some people sold tickets for the performances.

All these people went to the manager's party. The dancers and the singers were excited. They were talking together in one part of the room. But they were not talking about the party. They were talking about the ghost in the Opera House.

A few of the singers and dancers had seen a strange man in the Opera House. The man always wore a black cloak. And he always wore a white mask over his face. He never spoke to anybody. The singers and dancers named him, 'The Phantom of the Opera'.

'Have you seen him?' a young dancer asked one of the singers.

'Yes, I saw him last week,' the singer replied.

'Tell me about him,' said the dancer.

'He was tall and thin,' said the pretty singer. 'He

14

was wearing a black cloak.'

'Was he ugly or was he handsome?' asked the dancer.

'I don't know,' the singer said. 'He was wearing a white mask over his face. There were two holes in the mask, but I couldn't see his eyes.'

'Were you frightened?' asked the dancer.

'Yes, I was very frightened!' said the singer quickly. Her eyes were shining. She was excited.

'Have many people seen the ghost?' her friend asked.

'Madame Richard knows about him,' the singer said.

'Madame Richard told me about him. She said, "Every evening, the Phantom sits in Box Number 5. He watches the opera. I give him a programme and he pays me for it – he gives me 20 francs." She isn't frightened!'

At that moment, Madame Richard came into the room. Madame Richard was a ticket-seller. Every evening, she sold tickets for the performance at the Opera House. And she sold programmes to the people in the audience. Madame Richard was a very large woman with a loud voice. All the singers and dancers were frightened of her.

'Are you talking about the ghost again?' Madame Richard asked.

'Yes, yes!' said the young dancer. 'Please tell us about him. Does he always sit in Box Number 5?'

'I don't sell any tickets for Box Number 5,' said Madame Richard. 'But somebody *sits* in Box Number 5. He doesn't go into the box through the door. And nobody sees him. He's a ghost – a phantom!'

'Do you sell a programme to him?' asked the dancer.

'Yes, he always wants a programme,' said Madame Richard. 'Every evening, I put a programme on a chair in Box Number 5. Every evening, the programme disappears. And after the performance there is always 20 francs on the chair.'

'Oh! Does the Phantom of the Opera have money?' asked one of the other singers. 'Is he a rich phantom?'

'Yes, Yes! He is rich,' said Madame Richard. 'The Phantom is a gentleman. He wears fine clothes.'

'But you haven't seen him! You don't know about his clothes!' said the singer.

Suddenly, somebody knocked on the door of the room. The dancer opened the door. A tall, thin man stood in the corridor. He was wearing beautiful black clothes. The dancer screamed.

'The Phantom!' she shouted. 'It's the Phantom!'

Her friends laughed. 'That's not the Phantom,' one of them said. 'That's the Persian.'

The tall, thin man looked at the dancer. 'Where is Carlotta?' he asked quietly. 'Is she here?'

The dancer pointed along the corridor. She pointed to another door. 'Carlotta is in her dressing-room,' she said. 'Carlotta is very tired this evening. She will not come to the party.'

'Thank you,' said the thin man.

The dancer closed the door quickly. 'Who is that man?' she asked her friends.

'He is the Persian,' one of the singers said. 'He is a friend of the Phantom!'

Everybody laughed.

3

Raoul Goes to the Opera

In 1890, Raoul was twenty-one. He was a handsome and intelligent young man. In the spring, he went to Paris. He was going to live there with his brother, Philippe.

Philippe was forty-one. He was a rich and important man. He knew many important people in Paris. He knew the manager of the Opera House. And he knew many famous singers.

One evening, Philippe spoke to his brother.

'We will go to the Opera House tonight, Raoul,' he said. 'My favourite singer is going to sing tonight. She is very famous. Her name is Carlotta.'

'Everybody knows about Carlotta,' said Raoul. 'She is a very famous singer. I want to hear her voice.'.

'You will hear her tonight,' said Philippe. 'And you will meet Carlotta tonight,' said Philippe. 'I will take you to her dressing-room. I often visit the singers after the performance. I often go to their dressing-rooms.'

The two brothers went to the Opera House. But they did not hear Carlotta that evening. Carlotta did not sing. She was ill. That evening, a different singer performed. This singer was a very young woman. She had fair hair and blue eyes. She was very beautiful. And she sang very beautifully.

The people in the audience were excited. They

clapped their hands. They cheered loudly.

'Who is that singer?' asked Philippe. 'She has a wonderful voice.'

Raoul looked at the young woman on the stage.

'I know her,' he said. 'And you know her too, Philippe! Do you remember the girl on the beach – the girl in Brittany? She sang for me. She was on the beach with her father. I took her scarf from the sea. My clothes were wet and you were angry with me.'

'Yes, I remember,' said Philippe. 'The girl's father played the violin on the beach. And the girl sang. But I have not heard her sing here, at the Opera House. She's a very good singer!'

All the people in the audience liked the young singer very much. At the end of the performance, they clapped their hands and they cheered again.

After the performance, Raoul and Philippe met the manager of the Opera House.

'What is that young singer's name?' Philippe asked.

'Her name is Christine,' said the manager. 'She has a wonderful voice. One day, I heard Christine singing in the street. She sang very well. I brought her to the Opera House. She has a very good teacher. She is a very good singer. Soon, she will be famous. Tonight, Carlotta was ill. I said, "Christine will sing in the performance tonight." And she has sung beautifully.'

'I want to meet Christine,' Raoul said to Philippe. 'Please take me to her dressing-room.'

Philippe took Raoul to a corridor behind the stage. They were many doors in this corridor. They were the doors of the singers' dressing-rooms.

Many people were outside Christine's dressing-room. Everybody wanted to go into the room. Everybody wanted to speak to Christine.

The door of the dressing-room was open. But a man was standing in front of the door.

'I am a doctor,' he said to the people. 'You must not go into Christine's room. She must rest. She is very, very tired. Please go away.'

The other people went away. But Philippe knew the doctor. He spoke to the man. Then Philippe and his brother looked into the dressing-room. Raoul saw Christine. She was sitting on a chair. He smiled at her.

Suddenly, Christine saw Raoul. She stood up and she walked to the open door.

'Christine,' said the young man. 'My name is Raoul. I have seen you before. I saw you ten years ago. I saw you on a beach in Brittany. I took your scarf from the sea.'

'Yes, I remember that evening,' said Christine. 'I was ten years old. You ran into the sea. Your clothes were very wet. Your brother was angry!'

'Yes,' said Philippe. 'I was angry.' He smiled.

'You sang a song for me that evening,' said Raoul. 'And your father played his violin. Is your father well, Christine?'

'My father died last year,' Christine said sadly.

'I have often thought about you, Christine,' said Raoul. 'I want to meet you again.'

'I am very tired tonight,' said Christine. 'Please come another day.'

'I'll come tomorrow,' said Raoul.

'Please leave now,' said the doctor. 'Christine must rest!'

The doctor closed the door of the dressing-room.

———

A few minutes later, the two brothers were leaving the Opera House. They saw the manager again. He was standing outside the building. He was looking up at the stars in the dark sky.

'What is wrong with Carlotta?' Philippe asked him. 'Is she very ill?'

'No, she is not ill,' said the manager. 'But she is very worried. And she is very frightened. Now, she will not sing. She has seen the Phantom.'

'The Phantom? Do you believe that?' said Philippe.

'No! No! I don't believe it!' said the manager. 'But she saw somebody or something. Somebody or something frightened her.'

Philippe and Raoul said goodnight to the manager.

'Is there a ghost in the Opera House?' Raoul asked his brother.

'People like frightening stories,' said Philippe. 'And people tell foolish stories to each other. They talk about the Phantom of the Opera.'

4

Box Number 5

The next afternoon, Raoul went to the Opera House again. He went to the corridor behind the stage. He went to the door of Christine's dressing-room.

The door was closed. Raoul stopped outside the dressing-room. He heard two voices. Two people were speaking inside the dressing-room.

'You must always love me,' said a man's voice. 'You must sing only for me.'

'Yes. I will sing only for you,' said a woman's voice. It was Christine's voice. She said the words slowly.

Suddenly, the door opened. Christine came out of the dressing-room.

Raoul wanted to speak to Christine, but she did not see him. Her eyes were open, but she did not see Raoul! Was she asleep? The young man did not understand.

Christine walked quickly along the corridor and she went round a corner.

'Who was Christine speaking to?' Raoul asked himself. 'I want to know about him!'

The door of the dressing-room was open. Raoul looked into the room. But there was nobody in the dressing-room. It was empty!

———

In the evening, there was another party at the Paris Opera House. The manager invited Philippe and Raoul to the party. The party was in the restaurant at the Opera House. There were many famous and important guests at the party. First, they were going to enjoy the party. Then, they were going to watch a performance.

The guests ate and drank. The guests talked about Carlotta. They talked about Christine. And they talked about the Phantom of the Opera.

Raoul looked around the room. He saw a tall, thin man. The man was drinking a glass of wine. The man did not speak to anybody. But he looked at Raoul.

'Philippe, who is that tall, thin man?' Raoul asked.

'That's the Persian,' said Philippe. 'He's a strange man. He's very intelligent. Once, he was an architect. He helped the architect of the Paris Opera House. The Persian is often here in the evenings.'

Then the manager came towards Philippe and Raoul.

'Have you seen the Phantom?' Philippe asked him. 'Everybody is talking about the Phantom!' Philippe laughed.

'No, sir. I haven't seen him,' the manager replied angrily. 'But I know about the foolish stories. Madame Richard said to me, "The Phantom sits in a box every evening." And the Persian told me about the Phantom too!'

'I have met the Persian,' said Philippe. 'He is a very intelligent man. And I have heard the story about the box. Box Number 5 *is* empty every evening. Is that the Phantom's box?'

'Yes,' said the manager. 'Box Number 5 is always empty. People do not like Box Number 5. They say, "Box Number 5 is unlucky. That is the Phantom's box. The Phantom watches all the performances from Box Number 5." Well, I don't believe that! I have never seen the Phantom!'

'But Carlotta has seen the Phantom,' said Philippe. 'What did she tell you about him?'

'Oh, it was a very foolish story,' said the manager. She said, "The Phantom has a white face. It is the face of a dead man!" Everybody tells me this foolish story!'

'Do you believe Carlotta's story?' asked Philippe.

'No, no, I do *not* believe it,' said the manager. 'But Carlotta is very worried. I want to stop these stories. I want Carlotta to sing tonight. The Phantom's box –

Box Number 5 – will not be empty this evening. I have sold four tickets for Box Number 5.'

The party ended. All the guests left the restaurant. They were going to watch the performance.

———

Box Number 5 was not empty that evening. Two men and two women were sitting in the box.

Christine did not sing that evening. Carlotta sang in the opera. But Carlotta was worried. She did not sing very well. She often looked at Box Number 5.

The Opera House was lit brightly. There were many gas lights on the walls. And there were large glass chandeliers. The chandeliers hung from the ceiling. They hung above the audience.

At the end of the performance, there was a strange accident. The large chandelier near Box Number 5 fell suddenly. There was a loud crash – the sound of breaking glass. The four people in Box Number 5 were hurt by the broken glass. The glass hurt one of the women very badly.

After that evening, nobody bought tickets for Box Number 5. 'The Phantom is angry,' everybody said. 'Box Number 5 is the Phantom's box!'

After that, other strange things happened at the Paris Opera House.

Some scenery was broken.

A musician disappeared. Nobody could find him.

5

The Mirror in the Dressing-room

A week passed after the accident in Box Number 5. Raoul did not see Christine. She did not sing at the Opera House.

The young man was unhappy. He could not sleep at night. He was in love with Christine! He wanted to meet Christine. He was worried about her. What was wrong with her? Was she ill? And who was Christine's mysterious friend? Who was the man in the dressing-room? The man had a voice, but he had no body! Raoul wanted to meet him too!

One afternoon, Raoul went to the Opera House again. He asked one of the singers about Christine.

'Christine is not here now,' the singer said. 'But she will come soon.'

'I will wait for her,' Raoul said.

He went to Christine's dressing-room. The door was not locked. He opened the door and he went into the room.

The young man sat down on a chair, in a corner of the room. He waited for Christine.

Ten minutes later, the door opened. Christine came into the dressing-room. She closed the door behind her. Raoul looked at her. Again, the young singer did not see him. She looked at a large mirror on the wall of the dressing-room. Raoul was going to speak.

But suddenly, another man's voice spoke.

'Christine! Christine! Sing for me,' the voice said.
The voice had come from the mirror! And Raoul had
heard that voice before. He had heard it through the
door of the dressing-room!

Raoul looked at the big mirror on the wall. He did not understand.

Christine started to sing a song. She sang softly. She walked slowly towards the mirror. Suddenly, somebody knocked on the door of the dressing-room. There was somebody outside, in the corridor. Raoul turned his head. The young man looked at the door for a moment. Then he looked back at the mirror. But Christine had disappeared!

Raoul stood up and he ran to the mirror. He touched the glass. It was a heavy mirror. It was fixed to the wall.

'Where is Christine?' he thought. 'What shall I do?'

Raoul saw some writing paper and a pencil on Christine's table. Quickly, he wrote a note.

Christine
I was here. I saw you. Then you disappeared. I must meet you again. I love you. Please write to me, Christine.

Raoul

The young man put the note on Christine's table. Then he went back to his brother's house. Raoul was very unhappy. That night, he could not sleep. He thought about Christine. Where was she? Had she read his note?

A letter arrived for Raoul the next morning. The letter was from Christine! Raoul read it quickly.

Raoul

Come to the Opera House tomorrow night. There is going to be a grand ball there. Everybody is going to wear a mask. You must wear a white mask.

Do not show your face. Do not tell your name to anybody. At midnight, I will meet you at the ball.

Christine

In the afternoon, Raoul went to a shop near the Opera House. He bought a black cloak and a white mask. This was going to be his costume for the grand masked ball.

6

The Masked Ball

It was nearly midnight. Raoul was wearing his black cloak and his white mask. The young man looked around him. Hundreds of people had come to the grand masked ball at the Paris Opera House. Everybody was wearing a mask over their face. Raoul did not know anybody. And nobody knew him.

Raoul did not speak to anybody. He waited in a dark corner. Then he heard the bell of a clock. It rang twelve times. Midnight!

At that moment, a woman touched his arm. The woman was wearing a white cloak. Raoul could not see her face. She was wearing a black mask.

'Christine?' Raoul said. 'Are you Christine?'

The woman did not speak. She walked away from Raoul. Raoul followed her. The woman went behind the stage. She walked along a corridor. Then she started to climb some stairs. Raoul followed her up the stairs. They climbed many, many stairs.

At last, the woman stopped in front of a small door. She opened the door and she walked through it. Raoul followed her through the door. They were on the roof of the huge building. Raoul looked around him. He saw the lights of Paris below them.

The woman walked towards the edge of the roof. Then she stopped. Raoul walked towards her. They both took off their masks. Raoul saw Christine's face.

'Christine!' Raoul said. 'Christine, I love you! I saw you ten years ago, in Brittany. You sang for me and I loved you. The years passed. Then I saw you again and I loved you again! I came to the Opera House two days ago. I wanted to speak to you, Christine. I saw you in your dressing-room. But you disappeared. Where did you go, Christine?'

'You must not ask me that question, Raoul,' Christine said.

'But I love you!' said Raoul. 'Christine, please listen to me! Please sing for me again. Please marry me, Christine.'

'I cannot marry you, Raoul,' said Christine sadly.

'Why not, Christine? Why not?' Raoul asked.

'I cannot marry anybody,' Christine said. 'Erik will not let me get married.'

'Erik?' said Raoul.

'Erik is my Angel of Music,' Christine said. 'He is my teacher.'

'Tell me about Erik,' Raoul asked. 'Where is he?'

'Erik is an architect. He is a musician. And he is a wonderful teacher,' Christine said. 'He lives under the stage of the Opera House.'

'I want to meet him!' said Raoul. 'I want to speak to him!'

'No, Raoul, no!' said Christine. 'You must not speak to Erik.' Christine was frightened.

'I'm sorry, Raoul,' she said. 'I cannot get married. I cannot have friends. And I cannot sing for you again. I sing for Erik. I sing only for him. I will sing for him tomorrow night. I will sing in *Faust*.'

'Isn't Carlotta going to sing tomorrow?' Raoul asked.

'Carlotta will be ill again,' Christine said. 'Erik told me that. Erik knows everything!'

Suddenly, they heard a sound behind them. They were not alone on the roof. A tall man was standing near the door of the stairs. The tall man was wearing a black cloak and a white mask. He was looking at Raoul and Christine.

Christine was very frightened.

'Goodbye, Raoul, I must not meet you again,' she said. 'Goodbye!'

Then she ran away from the young man. She ran across the roof.

'Christine! Christine!' Raoul shouted. 'Where are you going? What shall I do?'

Raoul wanted to follow Christine. And he wanted to talk to the tall man in the white mask. Was this man Erik? And was Erik the Phantom of the Opera?

Raoul looked around him. Christine had gone. The tall man had gone too! Raoul was alone on the roof of the Opera House.

He looked up at the stars in the dark sky. He remembered the girl on the beach. The young man was very unhappy.

He walked slowly towards the stairs.

7

The Persian's Story

I am the Persian. I will tell you the second part of this story. It is the story of Christine and Raoul. But it is also the story of a strange man.

I know everybody at the Paris Opera House. And I know the building very well. I helped the architect of the Opera House. I know all the rooms there, and all the corridors and all the cellars.

I was a guest at the masked ball. I saw Raoul and Christine on the roof of the Opera House. I saw Christine run down the stairs. I saw Raoul walk down the stairs a few minutes later. I followed Raoul and I spoke to him.

'Raoul,' I said. 'You are very unhappy. You are in love with Christine. You are worried about her. I am worried about her too, Raoul.'

'Who are you?' asked Raoul.

'I am the Persian,' I said. 'You have seen me in the Opera House before.'

I took off my mask.

'Ah, yes,' Raoul said. 'Yes, the Persian. I have seen you at the Opera House. What do you want?'

'I want to help you,' I said.

'How? And why do you want to help me?' Raoul asked.

'There is great danger for Christine,' I said.

'What is the danger?' Raoul asked. 'Tell me, please!'

'Christine has a teacher,' I said. 'His name is Erik.'

'Christine told me about him. But who is Erik?' Raoul asked.

'I cannot tell you all of Erik's story,' I said. 'Erik has a secret. Once, Christine had a secret too. But Erik's secret is not Christine's secret.'

'I do not understand,' said Raoul.

'Erik's face is Erik's secret,' I said. 'And once, Christine could sing only for Erik. That was Christine's secret. But now, she can sing for everybody. And there is danger for her. We must help her!'

'What shall we do?' Raoul asked.

'We must take Christine away from Paris,' I said. 'We must take her away tomorrow. We must leave tomorrow night – after the performance. I will talk to

Christine.'

I looked at Raoul's face. He did not believe me. He walked away.

———

I am the Persian. I live in Paris now. But I was born in Tehran, in Persia.

Why did I come to France? I will tell you about that. Many years ago, I was following a very strange man. I followed him from Persia to France.

One evening, ten years ago, I was in Brittany. I was following the strange man along a beach. I saw him go into an old church. Then I saw Raoul and Christine on the beach. And I saw Philippe and Christine's father. I listened to them.

'I will send the Angel of Music,' Christine's father said.

And then Christine heard the sound of a violin.

'Is that the Angel of Music?' she asked.

I heard the sound too. It was coming from the old church. The sound was very, very beautiful. But a man was making the sound. He was not an angel!

8

Christine Disappears!

Raoul was an unhappy young man. He was in love. He did not want my help. But I – the Persian – understood his problems.

The morning after the masked ball, Raoul had breakfast with his brother. He told me about this, the next day.

'We will hear Carlotta sing tonight,' Philippe said.

'I want to go to the Opera House,' said Raoul. 'But I don't want to hear Carlotta. I want to hear Christine.'

'Do you like Christine very much?' Philippe said.

'Yes,' Raoul said. 'I love her, Philippe.'

That evening, the brothers went to the Opera House. There was a huge audience in the Opera House. They were waiting to hear Carlotta. There was going to be a performance of Gounod's opera, *Faust*. Carlotta was going to sing in this famous opera.

But Carlotta did not sing that night. Christine came onto the stage. At first, the audience was noisy. The people asked each other, 'Where is Carlotta?' But then Christine started to sing and the audience was quiet. They listened to Christine.

Christine sang beautifully. Her voice was strong and sweet. Everybody loved her voice. All the people in the audience clapped their hands and they cheered.

Raoul saw Christine standing on the stage. He saw

her beautiful fair hair and her beautiful blue eyes. He heard her wonderful voice. He loved her!

Soon, Christine walked to the front of the stage. She saw Raoul in the audience. She sang for him.

Angel of heaven, my angel of light,
Let us stay here on this beautiful night.

Suddenly, there was a loud noise. And suddenly, there was no light in the Opera House. The stage was dark. Christine stopped singing. The audience shouted angrily.

A few moments later, there was another noise. Then the stage was bright again. But Christine was not on the stage. She had disappeared!

The people in the audience stood up. They started to shout. The manager stopped the performance. What had happened? Where was Christine? Everybody wanted to hear her voice. But nobody could find the young singer.

The audience started to leave. The people were angry. Philippe and Raoul met the manager.

'What has happened?' Philippe asked him.

'Where is Christine?' Raoul asked.

'I do not know,' the manager replied. He was very worried. 'Christine has disappeared. She is not in the Opera House. I have sent for the police.'

———

Raoul and Philippe went home. Later, some policemen arrived at the Opera House. They talked to the manager. They talked to the ticket-sellers. They talked to the singers and the dancers. But they did not talk to me.

The policemen asked many questions. They walked through all the corridors of the Opera House. They went into all the rooms. They went into some of the cellars. Two hours passed. But the policemen did not find Christine.

'She has run away,' said a singer.

'She has a young friend,' said a dancer.

'Yes, his name is Raoul,' said Madame Richard. 'He lives in Paris. He lives with his brother.'

'Yes! Raoul has run away with Christine,' said another singer.

Raoul had not run away. He was at his brother's house. But Christine was not there. And Raoul was a very unhappy young man.

9

Under the Opera House

I am the Persian. I know the secrets of the Paris Opera House. And I know the secret of the Phantom of the Opera. Do you believe me? At first, Raoul did not believe me.

Christine disappeared from the Opera House. She was singing in *Faust*, but she disappeared! That night, the policemen went into all the rooms and corridors of the Opera House. They went into some of the cellars.

They did not find Christine. But they did not know the building well. They did not know about the trapdoors. And they did not know about the cellars on the other side of the lake! Soon, I will tell you about the trapdoors and the cellars and the lake.

The policemen did not find Christine. The next morning, I sent a note to Raoul. I waited for him. He came to my house in the afternoon.

'Where is Christine?' he asked. 'Is she here?'

'She is with Erik,' I said. 'She is with the Phantom of the Opera.'

'Will you take me to her?' Raoul asked.

'Yes, Raoul,' I replied. 'Come with me to the Opera House. We will find Christine.'

———

I took Raoul to the Opera House. We went behind the stage. We went into Christine's dressing-room.

46

'There are many secrets in the Opera House,' I said. 'Here is one of the secrets.'

I walked up to the large mirror on the wall. I touched the side of the mirror. The mirror was also a door. The door opened! Behind it, there was a dark corridor.

'Four days ago, Christine disappeared from this room,' Raoul said. 'I was here with her.'

He pointed at the chair in a corner of the room. 'I was sitting there,' Raoul said. 'Christine disappeared. I did not understand. But I understand now. The mirror is a door. Christine went behind that mirror.'

'There are many strange doors in the Opera House,' I said. 'And there are many trapdoors – doors in the floors. There is a trapdoor in the floor of Box Number 5. Erik goes to his box every evening through that trapdoor.'

'And there are trapdoors on the stage,' I said. 'Last night, Christine disappeared through a trapdoor in the floor of the stage.'

'Did Erik – the Phantom – take Christine away?' Raoul asked slowly.

'Yes,' I said. 'But Erik is not a ghost. Erik is a man.'

I took a lamp from the table. I lit the lamp and I walked into the dark corridor behind the mirror. Raoul followed me.

We came to some stairs. We stopped for a moment and we listened. We heard nothing! Then we walked down the stairs and we walked along some more dark corridors. Then we walked down some more dark stairs. We went down and down. We went very deep below the Opera House.

'Erik lives here, under the Opera House,' I said. 'We must be careful, Raoul. There are trapdoors in the floors. Sometimes the trapdoors open suddenly.'

'What do you know about Erik?' Raoul asked.

'Erik has a terrible secret,' I said. 'But he is a strange and clever man. In my country, we called him the Prince of Trapdoors.'

'Why did you give him that name?' asked Raoul.

'Once, Erik was a famous architect,' I said. 'Many years ago, he lived in Persia. He worked for the King of Persia. Erik was the architect of the famous Palace of Mazenderan in Persia. That building has many secrets too! There are many secret rooms and secret corridors. There are many secret doors and trapdoors.'

'Why did Erik come to France?' asked Raoul.

'He was unhappy in Persia,' I said. 'He finished his work at the Palace of Mazenderan. He wanted to leave Persia. He wanted to come to Paris. But the King wanted him to stay in Persia. Erik ran away. The King was angry.'

'And why did you come here?' Raoul asked.

'The King of Persia sent me to France,' I said. 'He said to me, "Find Erik! Erik knows all my secrets. Find him – then kill him!" I left Persia and I followed Erik.'

'But you haven't killed him,' Raoul said.

'No, I haven't killed him,' I answered. 'Erik is very clever. But he is very unhappy. I know Erik's secret. And I am sorry for him.'

'Why has he taken Christine away?' Raoul asked.

'Erik is a wonderful musician,' I said. 'And he is a wonderful teacher. He taught Christine about singing. But he taught her too well. Soon, she will be a famous singer. Once, she sang only for Erik. Now, she will sing for other people. Erik is unhappy about that. Erik loves Christine.'

'But I love Christine too,' Raoul said. 'I must take her away from Erik.'

'Erik wants her to stay with him,' I said. 'Once Erik was her only friend. She sang only for him. But last night, she sang for you. Erik is very angry!'

'Does Christine want to stay with Erik?' Raoul asked.

'We will ask her that question soon,' I replied.

10

The Lake and the Tree

I am the Persian. I know all the secrets of the Opera House. I know all the stairs and corridors under the stage. Raoul walked behind me. But our journey was dangerous. The light from my lamp was not bright. We walked through many dark places.

After ten minutes, we were in the deep cellars under the Opera House.

On the sixth floor below the ground, we came to a very large cellar. The scenery for the operas was in this cellar. There was a huge grey castle. It was made of wood. There were wooden statues of horses and kings. There was a garden of red paper flowers and green wooden trees.

'The policemen came to this cellar,' I said to Raoul. 'They did not find Christine here. Then they turned round. They went back to the stage. But we must go on.'

We walked to the other end of the large cellar. There was a door in the wall. But the door was two metres above the floor. We walked up some stairs to this door.

'Here is the lake,' I said.

I opened the door and we looked into the next cellar. We could not see the floor of that cellar. It was covered by water.

The water came up to the bottom of the door. I held up the lamp. Raoul looked round the huge cellar.

'The cellar is a lake,' I said. 'The water is about two metres deep.'

'Where has all the water come from?' asked Raoul.

'The water comes from a river,' I said. 'Now we must cross the lake!'

There was a small boat near the door. Raoul and I got into the boat and I rowed the boat across the lake.

'Have you been here before?' Raoul asked me.

'I have been here once before,' I replied. 'I tried to find Erik. But he was not at home.'

On the other side of the lake, there was another door. The bottom of the door was a few centimetres above the water. I rowed the boat to the door. I opened the door and we got out of the boat. We went through the door and we walked along a short corridor. Then we went up some stairs. We walked into another large cellar.

'We must be quiet now, Raoul,' I said. 'We are close to Erik's house. It is in on the fifth floor below the ground.'

'And where is Christine?' Raoul asked.

'She is in Erik's house,' I said. 'Don't worry about Christine, Raoul. Erik will not hurt Christine. We will see her very soon. But we will not go to the front door of Erik's house.'

I found a trapdoor in the floor. I opened it and I looked into a dark hole in the floor.

'We must go down there, Raoul,' I said. 'There is another cellar down there. We will go through that cellar. Then we will go up through a trapdoor into Erik's house. I will go first. Hold the lamp, please.'

I sat on the edge of the hole and I put my feet and legs through into the darkness. Then I jumped down into the hole. I jumped onto a stone floor.

'Give me the lamp,' I called to Raoul. 'The hole is not deep. You must jump down.'

A few moments later, we were both standing on the stone floor.

Suddenly, there was a noise above our heads. I held

up the lamp. Somebody had closed the trapdoor!

'Erik saw us coming,' I said. 'We must be very care-ful now, Raoul.'

We looked around us. We were in a small cellar. There was a metal ladder on the wall at the other side of the cellar. Above the ladder there was another trap-door. Quietly, we climbed the ladder. I opened the trapdoor and we climbed up through it.

We came up into a very strange room. The room was circular. There were many mirrors on the wall. There was a metal tree in the middle of the room. And there was a dead man hanging from the tree! There was a rope round his neck.

We walked towards the tree. I looked at the dead man. I knew him.

'This is terrible!' I said to Raoul. 'This man was one of the musicians in the orchestra. He disappeared a week ago. Erik has killed this musician. Now I understand. Erik is mad!'

There was a loud noise behind us. We turned round quickly. Somebody had closed the trapdoor in the floor!

I ran to the trapdoor and I tried to open it. But it was locked!

I looked round the room. I looked at the mirrors on the walls. In every mirror, I saw Raoul and myself. And in every mirror, I saw the metal tree and the dead man! We could not leave the terrible room of mirrors.

We went to the metal tree. Raoul cut the rope and I laid the dead man on the ground.

Then I looked up. There was a metal grille in the ceiling of the circular room. There was a trapdoor in this metal grille. It was two metres above our heads. We could not touch it.

Light was coming through the metal grille. It was the light of gas lamps.

'We are in Erik's house,' I said quietly. 'He is in the

room above us.'

We looked up through the grille. We saw the wall of the room above us. There were two strange handles on the wall. They were large, metal handles. One handle had the shape of a bird with huge wings – an eagle. The other handle had the shape of a fish.

There were noises in the room above us. Suddenly, two people were looking down at us. They were looking down through the grille. One of them was a tall man. He was wearing a black cloak and a white mask. The other person was a beautiful young woman.

'Christine!' Raoul called out. 'Christine!'

Christine looked down through the metal grille. She said nothing.

'Christine,' Raoul called again. 'Who is this man?' He pointed at the tall man.

I answered Raoul's question. I spoke to the man in the white mask.

'Erik!' I shouted. 'You are mad! We want to leave this house. And we want to take Christine with us!'

'No, Persian! You cannot leave,' said Erik. 'I must kill you both! Christine will stay here. She is mine. Christine loves me.'

'Christine, is this true?' Raoul shouted. 'Do you love that man? Tell me, Christine!'

Erik started to laugh. We heard the laughter of a madman!

'Is it hot in that room?' he asked. His voice was cruel and mad.

What was the meaning of Erik's words? I was afraid!

Suddenly, Raoul walked to one of the mirrors. He touched it quickly.

'The mirrors are hot!' he said.

Then I understood Erik's question. The mirrors were very hot. The room was very hot. The mirrors were heating the room. We could not breathe easily. Raoul and I moved to the centre of the room. But we heard Erik's voice through the grille. He was talking to Christine. Christine was crying.

'Your friends will die. They will burn,' said Erik.

'But you can help them, Christine.'

'How can I help them?' asked Christine.

'You must choose, Christine,' Erik said. 'Choose me or choose your young lover! You must choose one of us. And you must choose the eagle or the fish.'

'I don't understand you,' said Christine.

'Look at the handles on the wall,' Erik said. 'The handles bring fire and water. You must turn one of the handles. The eagle brings fire. The eagle will make the mirrors hotter. Your friends will die. But they will die quickly. They will burn!'

'The fish brings water,' Erik said. 'The fish will take the heat from the mirrors. But the fish has a secret. Remember, Christine! A fish can breathe under water. But people cannot breathe under water!'

11

The Phantom of the Opera

The circular room was terribly hot. The mirrors were terribly hot. Raoul put his hand on the metal tree. He screamed. The tree was terribly hot too.

'Christine,' he shouted. 'We are burning!'

We looked up through the grille again.

'Christine,' Raoul said. 'Please help us.'

'Turn the fish!' Erik said to Christine. 'Save your friends!'

Christine went to the handles on the wall. She put her hands on the metal fish. She waited for a moment. Did she believe Erik's words? Quickly, she turned the handle. Suddenly, we heard a loud noise.

'Good!' said Erik. 'Good! But remember my words, Christine. The fish has a secret!'

After a few moments, the room was cooler. We could breathe easily again.

Then there was another noise. The trapdoor in our floor opened. But we could not leave the circular room through the trapdoor. The cellar under the trapdoor was full of water. And water was coming up through the trapdoor.

The water was coming into the circular room very fast. Soon the water came up to our knees.

'Stop the water, Erik!' I shouted.

We heard Erik's mad laughter again.

'Christine has saved you from the fire,' he said. 'But I will not save you from the water. You are going to die!'

'Erik!' I shouted. 'I saved your life – remember that! The King of Persia said to me, "You must follow Erik. And you must kill him!" But I didn't kill you, Erik – remember that!'

The water was coming into the room faster and faster. Soon, it came up to our arms. Christine was crying loudly.

'Christine! Please help us!' Raoul shouted again.

'Please save them, Erik,' Christine said. 'Please, bring a ladder for them. Open the trapdoor in this grille. Let them climb up out of the water.'

Erik said nothing. He was looking down at us through the grille. Then he started to laugh again. He was mad! I was sorry for Erik. I had saved his life. But he wanted to kill me. He wanted to kill Raoul. He was going to kill us. Then he was going to take Christine away!

'Christine!' I shouted. 'Have you seen Erik without his mask? Have you seen Erik's face? I have seen it. It is terrible!'

The water came up to our necks. We started to swim. But our heads touched the grille. More water was coming into the room. In a minute, we were going to drown.

Christine had heard my words. Erik was Christine's Angel of Music. But she had never seen his face!

She looked at Erik. She looked at Raoul. And she looked at me.

Suddenly, Christine pulled Erik's mask from his face. She looked at his face. I knew about Erik's face. I had seen Erik's face many times. But Christine had never seen it before! Was she going to scream?

Erik's face was white. His eyes were dark holes in the white face. He had no hair. He had no nose. His face was the face of a dead man! This was Erik's secret.

Christine did *not* scream! She put her hands on her own face. And Erik put his hands on his face too.

'Christine,' Erik said quietly. 'You have seen my face. Can you love me?'

'Yes, I can love you,' Christine said. 'I sang for you. You were my wonderful teacher. I will always love my teacher. But I love Raoul too. Please, Erik, save Raoul and the Persian.'

Erik looked at Christine. Suddenly he opened the trapdoor in the grille.

'I am doing this for Christine!' Erik shouted.

He held my hand and he pulled me up into the room above. I turned round and I pulled Raoul from the water. I pulled him into the room.

Raoul went to Christine. He held her in his arms.

Erik was standing next to the grille. The water was coming through the grille. It was coming into the room very fast. Soon, the water came over our feet.

Erik was talking to himself. 'We'll go away,' he said. 'We'll leave Paris. Christine and I will be happy. I have never been happy before.'

'Come,' I said to Raoul and Christine. 'We must leave quickly. We cannot stop the water. Erik is mad.'

Raoul and I followed Christine to some stairs. We ran up these stairs. Behind us, we heard the sound of the water. And we heard the sound of a violin. It was a sad and beautiful sound. I had heard that sound ten years before. I had heard it on a sandy beach in Brittany. Christine had heard the sound too.

At the top of the stairs, we stopped for a moment. I looked back.

The strange, unhappy man was playing his violin. The water was still coming into the room. It had come up to Erik's arms. He looked up at me and I saw his terrible face again.

A moment later, the sound of the violin stopped. The Phantom of the Opera was dead!

Raoul and Christine and I walked up through the rooms of Erik's strange house. We found some more stairs. We climbed up and up. At last, we came out onto the roof of the Opera House. Above us, we saw the stars in the dark sky.

Exercises

Making Sentences

Write questions for the answers.

1 *What did Christine and her father do?*
Christine and her father were travelling musicians.

2 *What* ....
Christine's father played the violin.

3 *Did* ....
No, Christine did not play a musical instrument.

4 *Where* ....
Christine and her father travelled through all the countries of
Europe.

5 *Why* ....
People loved Christine because she had a beautiful voice.

6 *How* ....
Christine was ten years old in 1880.

7 *Where* ....
Raoul met Christine on a beach in Brittany.

8 *Why* ....
Philippe was angry with Raoul because he got wet.

9 *What* ....
Christine's father said to her: 'I will send the Angel of Music
to you.'

10 *What* ....
They heard the sound of a violin from the old church.

Pronunciation: ch

The letters *ch* have three sounds in English:

1 / ʃ / as in *chandelier*
2 / k / as in *architect*
3 / tʃ / as in *church*

Write the words from the box in the correct column.

mechanic   machine   chapter   school   chips   chef
orchestra   Christine   change   choose   chauffeur

/ ʃ /	/ k /	/ tʃ /
chandelier	architect	church

Musical Instruments
Which of these instruments do the people below play? Write sentences.

piano   drums   violin   flute   cello   trumpet

1	violinist	A violinist plays the violin.
2	cellist	
3	flautist	
4	pianist	
5	trumpeter	
6	drummer	

The Persian's Story
Complete the gaps. Use each word in the box once.

> musician   father   Persian   violin   story   know   mask
> return   Opera   rooms   ground   architect   hiding
> terrible   angel   beach   Persia   Europe   strange   kill

I am called the ¹.............Persian............ . I will tell you a story. It is the

²...................................... of Raoul and Christine. Yes. But it is also the

story of a very strange man.

I ³...................................... everyone at the Paris ⁴......................................

House. I know the building very well. There are many

⁵...................................... and corridors in the Opera House. I know

them all. Half of the building is under the ⁶...................................... .

There are many cellars deep underground. There are dark and secret

corridors. I know the architect. The ⁷..

built secret rooms in the cellars. Why?

Why am I in Paris? I come from [8]...................................... . The King of

Persia sent me to [9].. . I followed a

[10].. man from Persia to France.

The man's name is Erik. He is an architect and a

[11].. . He is very clever, but he has a

[12].. secret. He wears a

[13]...................................... . No one can see his face.

Why did I follow Erik? The King of Persia told me to

[14]...................................... him. I have not killed him, so I cannot

[15].. to my home.

When did I first see Christine? About ten years ago I was in Brittany.

Erik was nearby. Erik was [16].. in an old

church.

I saw Raoul and Philippe on the [17].. . I saw

Christine and her old father. I heard her [18]..

say: 'The Angel of Music will come to you.'

Erik heard these words too. I heard the sound of a

[19].. . The sound was coming from the old

church. It was very beautiful and very sad.

'Is that the Angel of Music?' Christine asked.

It was not an angel. It was a man. And the man was certainly no

[20]...................................... .

Words From the Story 1

R	Y	C	R	S	H	C	N	N	M	C
X	E	G	L	P	X	A	L	G	Z	H
S	N	M	R	E	A	L	B	A	E	A
S	A	B	C	R	C	C	C	C	P	N
B	U	A	E	F	C	S	O	O	M	D
V	D	L	L	O	I	T	R	S	A	E
I	I	L	L	R	D	A	R	T	N	L
O	E	Q	A	M	E	G	I	U	A	I
L	N	S	R	M	N	E	D	M	G	E
I	C	U	B	F	T	X	O	E	E	R
N	E	P	T	F	T	C	R	S	R	M

Find words in the square with the meanings below. The numbers in brackets show the number of letters in each word.

1 something that happens by chance – often bad (8)...*ACCIDENT*...

2 people who listen to music in a theatre (8)...........................

3 a high class party with music and dancing (4)...........................

4 a room underground for storing things (6)...........................

5 a special lamp with many pieces of glass (10)...........................

6 to hit hands together to make a noise (4)...........................

7 a long passage inside a building (8)...........................

8 clothes; actors wear them on-stage in a theatre (8)...........................

9 person who controls a business (7)...........................

10 to act or sing in a theatre (7)...........................

11 where the players act or sing in a theatre (5)...........................

12 a musical instrument; it is played with a bow (6)...........................

Odd One Out

In each group of words, one is different. Circle the odd one out.

1	violin	cello	chess	piano	flute
2	cellist	piano	violinist	drummer	flute
3	singer	performer	actor	musician	theatre
4	teacher	opera house	church	castle	palace
5	tutor	architect	violinist	manager	chandelier
6	scenery	costumes	curtains	orchestra	stage

Grammar Focus: joining short sentences

Join the sentences using the *–ing* form of the second verb.

1   Erik saw us. He saw us when we came into the cellar.
    Erik saw us coming into the cellar.
    ....

2   We noticed the water. It flooded into the cellar.

    ....

3   We heard Erik. He laughed at us.

    ....

4   We watched Erik. He held Christine's hand.

    ....

5   We felt the cold water. It rose higher and higher.

    ....

Words From the Story 2

Unjumble the letters to find words from the story.

1   RECALL   *cellar*
                    ....

2   MEANRAG   ....

3 NIVOIL ....

4 SKAM ....

5 GATES ....

6 LALB ....

7 CENTACID ....

8 OAFSUM ....

9 RODORRIC ....

10 LAREDCHIEN ....

11 CENSERY ....

12 GLEAN ....

Now use the words above to complete the gaps.

1 Monsieur Sartor Engloux ran the Opera House. He was the
....

2 A .... is a musical instrument made of wood. It has strings.

3 The Opera House is a huge building. It has hundreds of rooms,
joined by many ....s.

4 You could not see the Phantom's face because he wore a ....

5 Everyone in Paris knew about Carlotta. She was a ....
singer.

6 One day a .... fell into Box Number 5. There was
glass everywhere.

7 There was another .... soon after, when some
scenery was broken.

8 One day the .... lights suddenly went out, and
   Christine disappeared.

9 There are many scenes in an opera. Each scene looks different.
   The background .... makes the scene look real.

10 An .... has wings and carries messages.

11 Everyone wore a mask at the grand .... in the Opera
   House.

12 Raoul and the Persian looked for Christine in the
   ....s underneath the Opera House.`

Published by Macmillan Heinemann ELT
Between Towns Road, Oxford OX4 3PP
Macmillan Heinemann ELT is an imprint of
Macmillan Publishers Limited
Companies and representatives throughout the world
Heinemann is a registered trademark of Pearson Education, used under licence.

ISBN 978-0-2300-3034-3
ISBN 978-1-4050-7634-0 (with CD pack)

This retold version by Stephen Colbourn for Macmillan Readers
First published 1998
Text © Stephen Colbourn 1998, 2002, 2005
Design and illustration © Macmillan Publishers Limited 1998, 2002, 2005

This edition first published 2005

Illustrated by Francisco Meléndez and Justo Núñez
Map on page 3 and illustrations on pages 6 and 7 by John Gilkes
Original cover template design by Jackie Hill
Cover photography by Thinkstock/Getty
Acknowledgements: The publishers would like to thank Mary Evans
Picture Library for permission to reproduce the picture on page 4.

Printed in Thailand

2012   2011   2010
8   7   6   5   4

with CD pack

2013   2012   2011
19   18   17   16   15